SPMG
SSMG

HEINEMANN MATHEMATICS 7

Extension textbook

These are the different types of pages and symbols used in this book:

7
Handling data 1:
Construction of
bar graphs

These pages develop mathematical skills, concepts and facts in a wide variety of realistic contexts.

17
Extended
context

Extended contexts require the use of skills from several different areas of mathematics in a section of work based on a single theme.

33
Detour:
Distance tables

Detours provide self-contained activities which often require an exploratory, investigative approach drawing on problem-solving skills.

Challenge

Challenges are more-demanding activities designed to stimulate further thought and discussion.

HEINEMANN
EDUCATIONAL

Contents

This shape is called a Star of David. This page shows you how to make it and other stars.

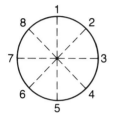

1 (a) Draw a circle of radius 5 cm and cut it out.
   (b) Fold it in half, in half again, and then again.
   (c) Open it out and use a ruler and a pencil to join the points 1 to 2, 2 to 3, 3 to 4, 4 to 5, 5 to 6, 6 to 7, 7 to 8, and 8 to 1.
   (d) Cut out the shape and name it.

2 (a) Draw another circle of radius 5 cm and cut it out.
   (b) Fold it as you did in question **1** and open it out.
   (c) Join the points 1 to 4, 2 to 5, 3 to 6, 4 to 7, 5 to 8, 6 to 1, 7 to 2, and 8 to 3, to draw an eight-pointed star.
   (d) Colour your star.

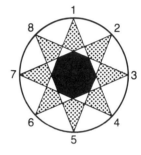

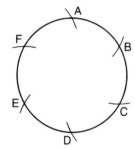

3 (a) Draw a circle with radius 8 cm.
   (b) Keep the compasses set at 8 cm. Start with centre A and mark off six points on the circumference. (A, B, C, D, E, F in the diagram.)
   (c) Join the points A to B, B to C, C to D ..., F to A.
   (d) Cut out this shape and name it.

4 You can make all these designs by drawing circles and marking off the circumferences as in question **3(b)**.

   (a) Try making these designs with circles of radius 6 cm.

   (b) Make a greetings card or a mobile.

   Make the circles 6 cm radius for the card and 10 cm radius for the mobile.

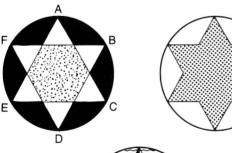

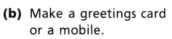

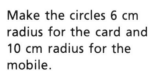

You often see symmetrical patterns on wall or floor tiles.
You can make your own symmetrical patterns:

You need three different coloured pencils – colours 1, 2 and 3 – and squared paper.

1 (a) Copy each grid on squared paper and colour the numbered squares.
   (b) Colour other squares so that each completed pattern has the lines of symmetry shown.

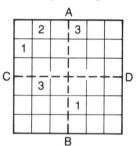 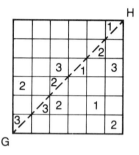 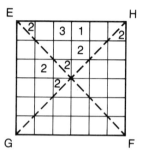

2 Copy each grid on squared paper. Choose squares to colour so that each completed pattern has only the lines of symmetry shown here.

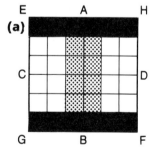 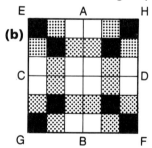 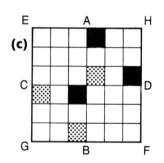

3 Name the lines of symmetry for each of these grid patterns.

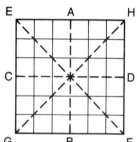 **(a)**   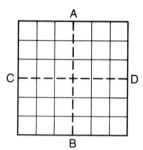 **(b)**   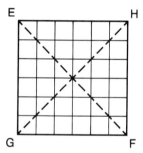 **(c)**

4 Which of these equilateral triangle patterns are symmetrical?
   Name their lines of symmetry.

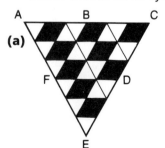 **(a)**   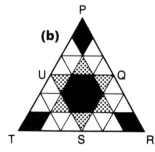 **(b)**   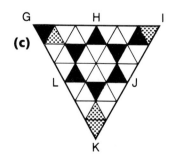 **(c)**

Large wall patterns

You can't always tell what designs will look like in real life.
Enlarge a tile design to life size and make a wall display:

Work in a group.

1 Each one of you should use three
colours to make a 36-square pattern
with **four** lines of symmetry.
A shows a sample pattern.

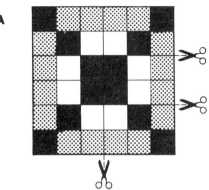

A

2 Your group should choose only **one** of
the patterns to enlarge for a wall
display. Cut up this pattern into **six**
parts as shown in **B**.

B

3 Now enlarge each of the six parts.
- Draw a rectangle 27 cm by 18 cm,
  on plain paper.
- Cut out the rectangle.
- Divide it into six squares.
- Colour these squares to complete
  your enlargement.
  C shows a sample enlargement.

4 Paste each of the six coloured
enlargements in its correct position on
a large sheet of paper.

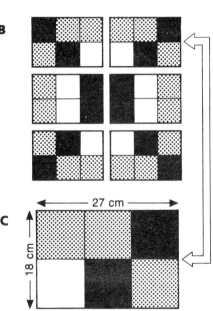

C

27 cm

18 cm

Work in a group.

5 (a) How many lines of symmetry has the shaded pattern of
equilateral triangles shown in **X**?

(b) Your group can make a large copy of this pattern for a
wall display. Make 24 large equilateral triangles.
- Draw a circle with radius 9 cm on plain paper.
- Use the method described on page **1**, question **3(b)**,
  to mark off six points on the circumference.
- Join the six points to make six equilateral triangles as
  shown in **Y**.
- Cut out the triangles.
- Colour the triangles and fit them together to complete
  the large copy.

X

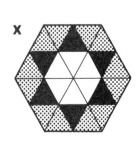

Y

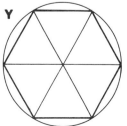

Ask your teacher what to do next.

Cars and racetracks

Use a calculator if you wish.

1 The scale of this model car
is **1 cm to 36 cm.**
What is **(a)** the true height
(b) the true length?

2 These two models are made to the scale **1 cm to 64 cm.**

(a) What is the difference between the true lengths?
(b) What is the difference between the true heights?

3 Ask your teacher if you can collect models whose scales you
know. Find the true length of each.

This car racing circuit is divided into six sections.
The scale of the plan is **1 cm to 50 m.**

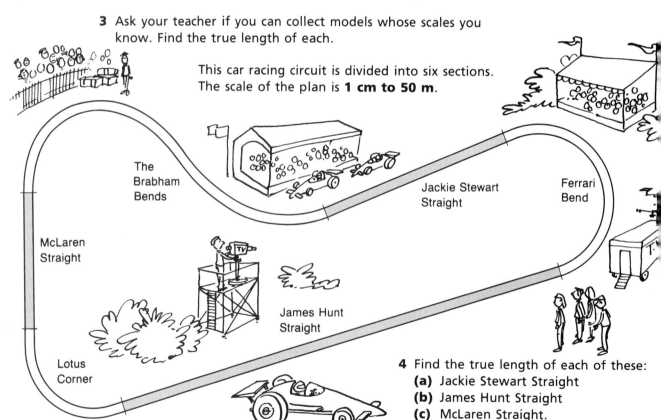

The
Brabham
Bends

McLaren
Straight

Jackie Stewart
Straight

Ferrari
Bend

James Hunt
Straight

Lotus
Corner

4 Find the true length of each of these:
(a) Jackie Stewart Straight
(b) James Hunt Straight
(c) McLaren Straight.

5 Find the true distance round each of these:
(a) Ferrari Bend **(b)** Lotus Corner **(c)** the Brabham Bends.

6 (a) Find the approximate distance, in kilometres, for one lap of the track.
(b) A race is 76 laps of this track. About how many kilometres is this?

Here are Jim's sketches, **not** to scale, of some buildings. He has marked the true measurements.
He wants to make models of the buildings to the scale **1 cm to 50 cm**.

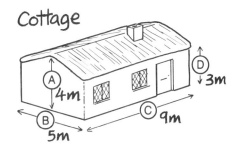

Cottage

He calculates the scaled length for A like this:
  50 cm is represented by 1 cm
400 cm is represented by 400 ÷ 50
      = **8 cm**

The scaled length for A is **8 cm.**

1 Find the scaled lengths for each of the measurements B, C, D, ..., K.

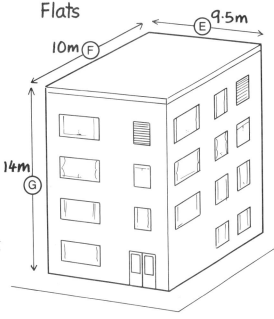

Flats

Semi-detached houses

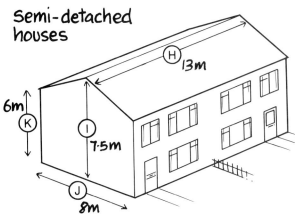

2 Work with a partner to make a model of the cottage.

(a) Half of the gable end of the cottage is drawn here.
Each make one complete gable end and one of the other walls of the cottage, using a scale of **1 cm to 50 cm**.

(b) Make a roof for the cottage.

(c) Stick your pieces together to make the model cottage.
Stick on a door and windows if you wish.

Ask your teacher what to do next.

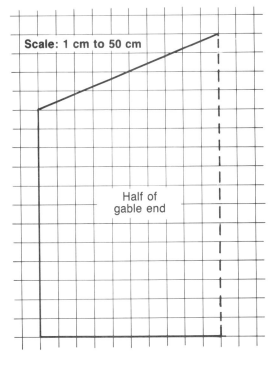

Scale: 1 cm to 50 cm

Half of gable end

Keeping warm

Fuel costs

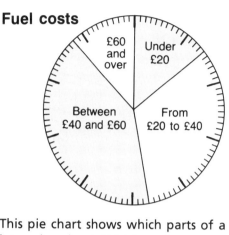

1 This pie chart gives information about the average monthly fuel costs for heating in 100 houses. How many houses had costs
(a) under £20
(b) from £20 to £40
(c) between £40 and £60
(d) of £60 and over?

2 This pie chart shows which parts of a house lose heat. Which part
(a) loses most heat
(b) loses least heat?

3 What percentage of the heat is lost through
(a) the floor
(b) the roof, windows and draughts altogether
(c) the walls?

4 What fraction of the heat is lost through
(a) the roof **(b)** draughts
(c) the floor
(d) the walls and the floor together?

5 Use the 'Heat loss' information to make a **bar graph** showing the percentage of heat each part of the house loses.

6 Compare the pie chart with your bar graph.
Which shows more clearly that one quarter of the heat is lost through draughts and windows together?

Heating fuels

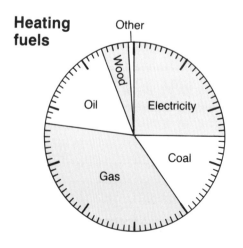

7 This pie chart shows the main fuels that 100 houses use for heating.
Draw a **bar graph** to show the same information.

8 Compare the pie chart with your bar graph.
Which shows more clearly
(a) the number of houses which use each fuel
(b) that one quarter of the houses use electricity
(c) that more of the houses use oil than use coal
(d) that more than half of the houses use either gas or oil?

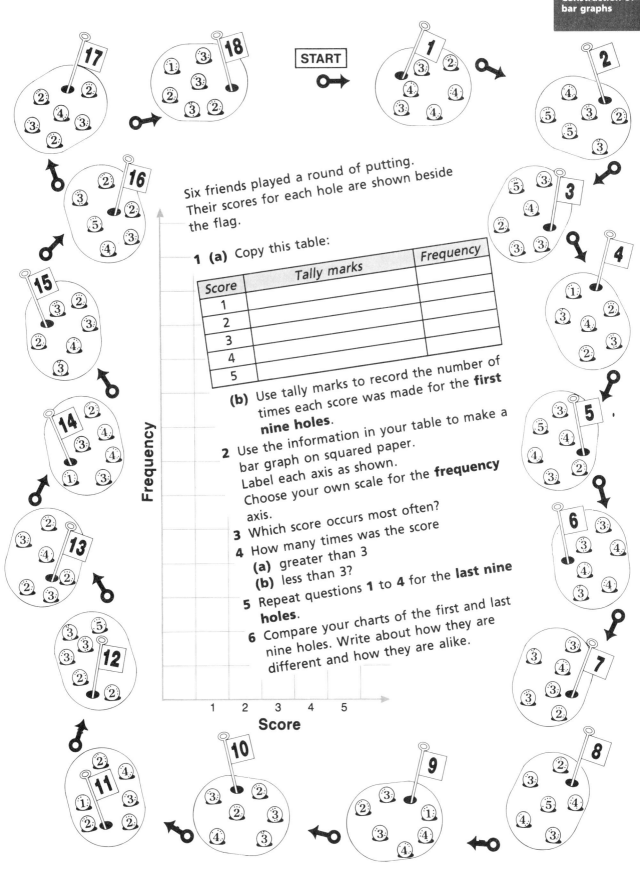

Six friends played a round of putting.
Their scores for each hole are shown beside
the flag.

1 (a) Copy this table:

Score	Tally marks	Frequency
1		
2		
3		
4		
5		

(b) Use tally marks to record the number of
times each score was made for the **first
nine holes**.

2 Use the information in your table to make a
bar graph on squared paper.
Label each axis as shown.
Choose your own scale for the **frequency**
axis.

3 Which score occurs most often?

4 How many times was the score
  (a) greater than 3
  (b) less than 3?

5 Repeat questions **1** to **4** for the **last nine
holes**.

6 Compare your charts of the first and last
nine holes. Write about how they are
different and how they are alike.

Frequency

Score

Ask your teacher what to do next.

Domino squares

You need these eight dominoes.

1

6	6	3	6
6	6	4	4
5	5	3	5
5	5	3	4

← You can make this number square by arranging the dominoes like this. ➡

Make the number square using a **different** arrangement of the dominoes.

2 Arrange the dominoes to make each of these number squares.
Make up your own method of recording your arrangement.

(a)

6	4	5	5
4	5	6	5
6	6	3	3
4	3	5	6

(b)

5	6	4	6
5	6	6	5
5	3	6	4
3	5	4	3

(c)

3	5	4	5
6	5	3	5
6	6	4	5
4	3	6	6

(d)

6	6	5	4
3	5	4	5
6	6	3	5
4	3	6	5

(e)

4	3	4	5
6	5	6	4
6	5	5	6
5	3	6	3

(f)

3	5	6	6
6	4	4	6
5	5	3	3
4	6	5	5

Try to find another arrangement for each square.

For which square is there only one possible arrangement?

Ask your teacher what to do next.

You can add numbers in any order.

1 Find out if what Steve says is true for these additions:
(a) 32 + 29 + 47
(b)   94   **(c)**   51   **(d)**   4·9
      63   86   8·3
    + 75   + 18   + 5·8

Check some additions of your own.

2 Find out if what Lisa says is true for these subtractions:
(a) 432 − 179   **(b)** 504 − 286
(c) 624 − 356   **(d)** 8·17 − 5·68

Check some subtractions of your own.

If you add the answer to the smaller number, you get the number you started with.

3 (a) Find: ● 7 × 8 and 8 × 7
           ● 9 × 13 and 13 × 9
           ● 14 × 16 and 16 × 14
(b) What do you notice?
(c) Write a statement about multiplying two numbers together.

4 (a) Find: ● 3 × 4 × 5, 4 × 5 × 3 and 5 × 3 × 4
           ● 8 × 7 × 9, 7 × 9 × 8 and 9 × 8 × 7
(b) What do you notice?
(c) Write a statement about multiplying three numbers together.
(d) Find out about multiplication with four numbers and write a statement about it.

You can check a division by multiplying your answer and the number you divided by.

5 Find out if what Aziz says is true for these divisions:
(a) 48 ÷ 3   **(b)** 112 ÷ 4   **(c)** 222 ÷ 6

Check some divisions of your own.

6 Some divisions have remainders. Find a way of checking divisions like these:
(a) 67 ÷ 5 = 13 r 2   **(b)** 214 ÷ 9 = 23 r 7

Write a statement about checking divisions with remainders.

7 Ask a partner to check your statement with these divisions:
(a) 318 ÷ 4   **(b)** 229 ÷ 7   **(c)** 370 ÷ 8

Challenge

Ask your teacher what to do next.

Sometimes you need to split up shapes to find their areas.

1 This drawing shows the measurements of a shape.
It is divided into two rectangles, **P** and **Q**.

Copy and complete:

Area of rectangle **P** = ▪ cm²

Area of rectangle **Q** = ▪ cm²

Area of **whole** shape = ▪ cm²

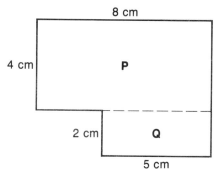

2 In the same way, find the area of each shape:

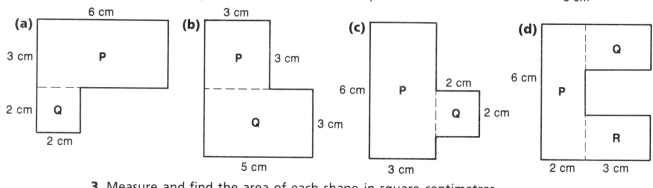

3 Measure and find the area of each shape in square centimetres.

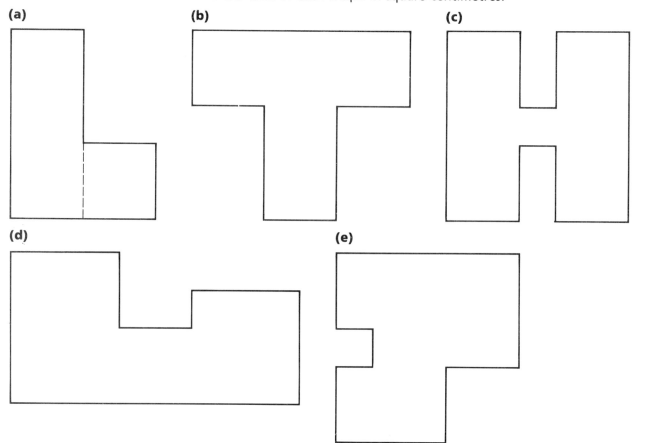

4 On cm squared paper, draw 'letters' which each have an area of 12 cm².

1 This trapezium shape has been divided into a
rectangle and two right-angled triangles, **X** and **Y**.
Copy and complete:

Area of rectangle = ▧ cm²

Area of triangle **X** = ▧ cm²

Area of triangle **Y** = ▧ cm²

Area of trapezium = ▧ cm²

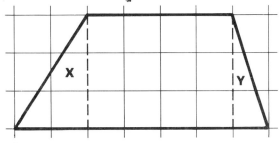

2 In the same way, find the areas of these shapes:

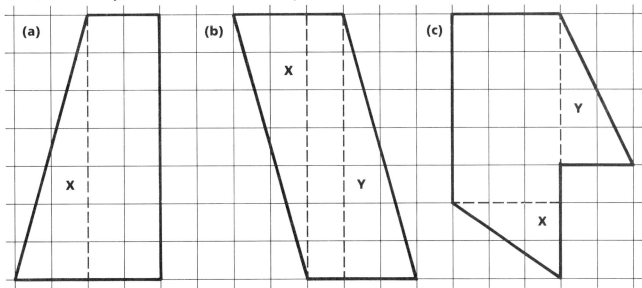

(a)

(b) **X** **Y**

(c) **Y** **X**

3 Find the area of each of these shapes:

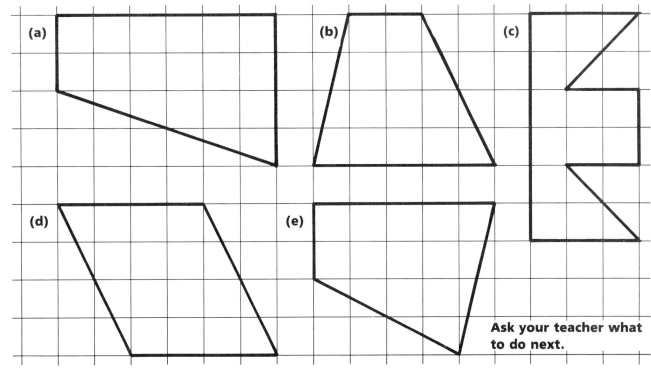

(a)

(b)

(c)

(d)

(e)

**Ask your teacher what
to do next.**

Costs and wages

What is the cost of **one** strawberry plant when you buy a box of 15?

No. of plants	Cost in £
15	10·50
1	10·50 ÷ 15 = 0·7

Enter `10.50` Press `÷` `1` `5` `=` to give `0.7`

The cost of a single plant is **£0·7** or **70p**.

STRAWBERRY 15 for £9·75

RASPBERRY 25 for £24·75

BLACKCURRANT 45 for £49·50

1 Find the cost of **one** plant in each of the boxes above.

2 How much cheaper is one plant from each of these boxes than the single plant?

£1·30 each GOOSEBERRY box of 18 £22·50

£1·60 each BLACKBERRY box of 12 £17·40

£1·90 each REDCURRANT box of 24 £42

Geraldine picks fruit. She earns £1·92 for collecting 12 kg of strawberries.
How much will she earn for 14 kg?

Weight in kg	Pay in £
12	1·92
1	1·92 ÷ 12 = 0·16
14	0·16 × 14 = **2·24**

Enter `1.92` Press `÷` `1` `2` `=` to give `0.16` → Do **not** clear the calculator

Press `×` `1` `4` `=` to give `2.24`

Or Enter `1.92` Press `÷` `1` `2` `×` `1` `4` `=` to give `2.24`

She will earn **£2·24**.

3 Find **(a)** $(8·84 ÷ 17) × 13$ **(b)** $(2·73 ÷ 21) × 53$ **(c)** $(9·8 ÷ 14) × 18$ **(d)** $(14·35 ÷ 35) × 50$

4 Here are some berry pickers' pay slips.

How much would Tom earn for collecting
(a) 17 kg of strawberries
(b) 18 kg of blackcurrants
(c) 11 kg of gooseberries
(d) 26 kg of blackberries
(e) 23 kg of blackcurrants
(f) 20 kg of strawberries?

PICKER: Jackie
FRUIT: 12 kg strawberries
PAY: £1·92

PICKER: Awaz
FRUIT: 13 kg blackcurrants
PAY: £2·21

PICKER: Fiona
FRUIT: 22 kg blackberries
PAY: £2·86

PICKER: Alan
FRUIT: 19 kg gooseberries
PAY: £2·85

Ask your teacher what to do next.

Nina wound up a clockwork model motor boat *Kitty* and put it in a boating pond. The line graph shows the distances it had travelled after certain times.

1 What does one small interval represent on
(a) the time axis
(b) the distance axis?

2 How long did it take the boat to travel
(a) 15 metres
(b) 10 metres
(c) 12 metres?

3 How far had the boat travelled after
(a) 20 seconds
(b) 14 seconds
(c) 44 seconds?

Kitty's journey

(graph: Distance in metres vs Time in seconds)

4 How far had the boat travelled after
(a) 80 seconds **(b)** 90 seconds **(c)** 100 seconds?

5 (a) What do you notice about your answers to question **4**?
(b) Suggest a reason for this.

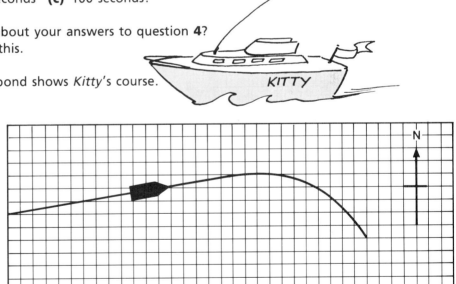

KITTY

6 This plan of the boating pond shows *Kitty*'s course. The breadth of the pond is 8 metres.
(a) What length is represented by each small interval?
(b) What is the length of the pond?

7 What was the closest distance *Kitty*'s course came to
(a) the North edge
(b) the South edge
(c) the East edge of the pond?

N

8 Max sailed his model boat *Hawk* on the pond. This table shows how far *Hawk* had travelled at various times.

Time in seconds	0	20	40	60	80	100	120	140
Distance in metres	0	10	16	19	21	22	22·5	22·5

Draw a line graph of this information.

Afternoon cruises

Each afternoon the motor launch *Seamist* sails from Oran to the islands of Rona and Kerry.

The graph shows *Seamist*'s journey.

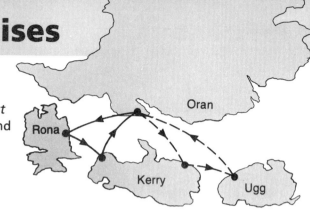

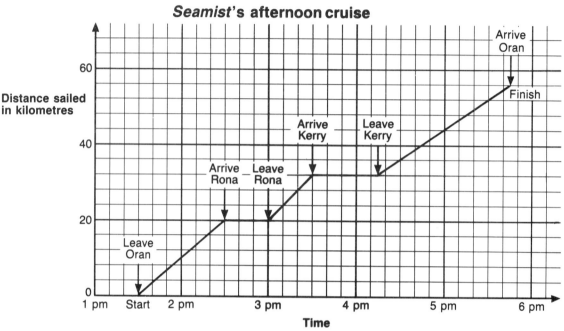

Seamist's afternoon cruise

1 What does one small interval represent on
  (a) the time axis   **(b)** the distance axis?

2 At what time did the cruise
  (a) start   **(b)** arrive at Rona   **(c)** leave Rona
  (d) arrive at Kerry   **(e)** leave Kerry   **(f)** finish?

3 For how long did *Seamist* stay at   **(a)** Rona   **(b)** Kerry?

4 How far had *Seamist* travelled when she   **(a)** arrived at Rona
  (b) left Rona   **(c)** arrived at Kerry   **(d)** left Kerry?

5 How far did *Seamist* sail   **(a)** between Rona and Kerry
  (b) altogether during the afternoon cruise?

6 The motor launch *Seaspray* sails from Oran to the islands of Kerry and Ugg.

Here is the timetable for *Seaspray*'s cruise.
Use this information to draw a graph of *Seaspray*'s journey.

Island cruise aboard *Seaspray*

	Leave Oran	Arrive Kerry	Leave Kerry	Arrive Ugg	Leave Ugg	Arrive Oran
Time	1 pm	2 pm	2.30 pm	3.10 pm	4 pm	5.15 pm
Distance from start	0 km	20 km	20 km	36 km	36 km	60 km

Boats for hire

1 The tourist board at Oran publishes a leaflet about hiring boats. The graph shows how much two companies charge for yacht hire.

For **each** company, how much does it cost to hire a yacht for
(a) 3 hours
(b) 8 hours?

2 What advice would you give a friend who wishes to hire a yacht?

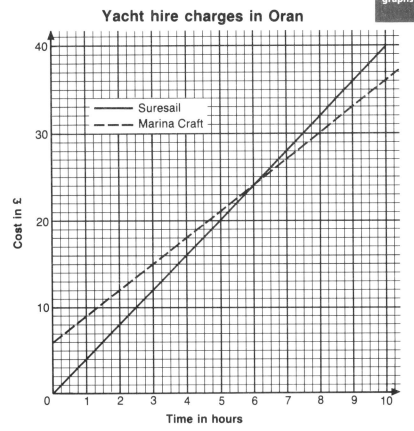

Yacht hire charges in Oran

- Suresail
- - - Marina Craft

Cost in £ / Time in hours

3 (a) Copy and complete these tables.

Time in hours	2	5	10
Cost in £			

Time in hours	2	5	10
Cost in £			

SURESAIL BOATS
POWER BOATS – FOR HIRE –
£8 per hour

MARINA CRAFT
POWER BOAT
£12 plus £5 per hour

(b) Draw a graph for the tourist board's leaflet like the one above to show **Power boat hire charges** in Oran.

4 Use your graph.
(a) Which company charges less for ● 3 hours ● 8 hours?
(b) What advice would you give a friend who wishes to hire a power boat?

Ask your teacher what to do next.

Marquees and tents

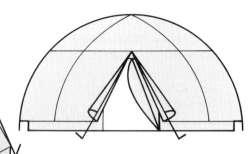

Instructions for making a three-dimensional shape from a net

- Copy the net on cm squared paper.
- Glue the net to card and cut it out.
- Fold along the dotted lines so that the card is on the **outside**
- Join edges with sticky tape.

Work with a partner.

1 (a) Follow the instructions and each make a three-dimensional shape from this net.

(b) Colour the **card** surface of rectangle R green.

(c) Glue the green rectangles together to make a marquee shape.

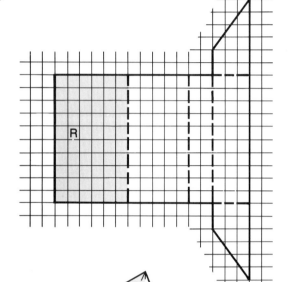

The marquee is **balanced** about the joining wall made by the green rectangles.

The rectangular joining wall is a **plane of symmetry.**

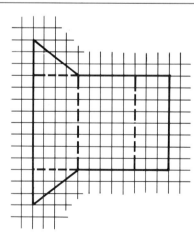

2 (a) Make three three-dimensional shapes each from this net.

(b) Glue the shapes together in pairs to make **three** different tent shapes, each with a **plane of symmetry**.

Ask your teacher what to do next.

The School Concert

Gladeside School organised a concert to raise money for the school fund. The school decided to spend the money raised on one or more of these items.

SUPERB BUY

£520

£129

£460

£125

RADIO CASSETTE RECORDER

Credi

Work in a group.

1 *Pupils wrote suggestions to help make the concert a success. These are some of their ideas. Discuss them and write some of your own.*

> I think we should run a raffle with a very good prize.

> We could make a lot of fudge and sell it during the interval.

> A pop star at our concert would attract a lot of people.

> Some of the shops in the town might be sponsors for our concert.

> We could make large posters to display in shop windows.

> Let's make beautiful decorations for the school hall.

2 *Copy this **profits table** to use with pages 18 to 22.*

Profits Table	
School fund balance	£148·00
Ticket sales	
Programme sales	
Kiosk profits	
Guess the weight of the cake	
Chocolate raisin slices	
Donations	£25·00
Grand total	

How many seats in the hall?

1 Work in a group.

A group of pupils at Gladeside wanted to find how many chairs they could fit into their school hall. They investigated how to arrange the chairs. You try this.

(a) Set out a few chairs in a row as shown, so that people can sit comfortably. Measure in centimetres how much room, **X**, each person should have.

(b) Now set out the chairs one behind the other, so that people have enough knee room. Remember that people will have to move between the rows. Measure the distance, **Y**, in centimetres.

2 The pupils at Gladeside discovered that they should allow 50 cm for each chair in a row and 100 cm between rows.
This means that **X** is 50 cm and **Y** is 100 cm.
Compare these results with your own.

3 The Gladeside pupils measured the dimensions of their school hall to the nearest metre.
They drew a plan of the hall using a scale of **1 cm to 2 m**. Their plan is shown on the opposite page.

(a) What is the true length and the true breadth of the hall?

(b) How broad is each passage?

(c) How broad and how long are the seating areas?

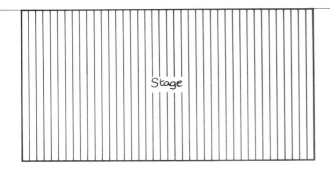

Gladeside School Hall

Scale : 1 cm to 2 m

☐ seating area

☐ passages

4 Use **X** = 50 cm and **Y** = 100 cm.

For **each** seating area in Gladeside School Hall, calculate
(a) the number of chairs in each row
(b) the number of rows of chairs.

5 How many people altogether can be seated in the hall?

6 An adult's ticket for the School Concert costs £1 and a child's ticket 60p.
All the seats were filled. 25% of the audience were children. How much did the school collect from the sale of tickets altogether?
Record this amount in your **profits table**.

7 (a) Measure the length and breadth of your own school hall to the nearest metre.
(b) Use cm squared paper and draw a plan of your hall using a scale of **1 cm to 2 m**.
(c) Draw in the seating area. Remember to leave passages 2 metres wide
  ● at the stage
  ● at the sides of the hall
  ● at the back of the hall
  ● down the middle of the hall.

8 How many people can be seated in your school hall when you use
(a) **X** = 50 cm and **Y** = 100 cm
(b) your own measurements for **X** and **Y** from question **1** opposite?

Programme planning

A group of pupils in Gladeside School were planning the concert programme. First they found out how long different kinds of concert items were likely to last.

1 Here are four concert items. Items requiring music are shown by ●.

The four items have to be arranged so that
★ the gymnastic display comes last
★ the choir does not appear first
★ musical and non-musical items are placed alternately
★ there is a one-minute interval between items.

Copy and complete a programme table like this for the four items.

Class	Item	Time in minutes
3	● Choir	6
5	● Dance team	5
4	Sketch	4
6	Gymnastic display	7

Class	Item	Duration
		7.15–

2 Here are the items for the first half of the Gladeside School Concert.
Items requiring music are shown by ●.

Make a programme table for the first half of the concert so that
★ the concert starts at 7.15 pm
★ Class 1 and 2 items are finished by 7.30
★ no more than two musical items are placed consecutively
★ the same class does not appear in two consecutive items
★ there is one minute for announcements between items and 2 minutes for arranging scenery before the play.

Class	Item	Time in minutes
1	● Singing Game – 'The Rainbow'	2
2	● Dance – 'Maggie's Movers'	4
3	● Festival Choir	6
5	● 'Mexican Carnival'	6
1	● Ballet – 'Animal Magic'	3
2	● Mime – 'Robots'	3
4	Sketch – 'Dad's Tea'	4
5	Play – 'Haunted House'	15

3 (a) Gladeside School sold 282 programmes at 20p each.
How much did they collect?
Insert this amount in your profits table.

(b) Design a cover for the programme and a ticket for the concert.

PRICE LIST

nuts	20p
coke	25p
orange	16p
apples	18p
crisps	15p

Carol and Carl ran the snacks kiosk at the School Concert.

1 Parents donated the nuts and apples. **Use the price list.**
  Carol and Carl sold 32 packets of nuts and 51 apples. Find how much money they collected.
  All of this money was **profit**.

2 **Use a calculator.** *Mr Jacobs bought crisps and Coke at a cash and carry.*

  A box of 48 packets cost £5·76   *A tray of 24 cans cost £5·28*

  Find the price of **(a)** *1 packet of crisps*   **(b)** *1 can of Coke.*

3 **Look at the price list.**
  How much profit did Carol and Carl make on
  (a) 1 packet of crisps   **(b)** 1 can of Coke?

4 At the concert, they sold 144 packets of crisps and 120 cans of Coke.
  What profit did they make from the sale of crisps and Coke?

5 **Work in pairs. You need a 2-litre bottle
  and a plastic cup.**
  Mr Jacobs bought orange in 2-litre bottles to
  pour into plastic cups.
  Find out approximately how many plastic
  cupfuls you get from a 2-litre bottle.

6 **Use the price list and your answer to
  question 5.**
  A 2-litre bottle of orange costs 99p.
  (a) How much profit did Carol and Carl
    make on each bottle?
  (b) Find **to the nearest penny** the **cost** of
    one plastic cupful.

7 At the concert Carol and Carl used eighteen 2-litre bottles of orange.
  What profit did they make from selling the orange?

8 *Use your answers from questions* **1**, **4** *and* **7** *to find the* **total** *profit
  Carol and Carl make in the concert kiosk. Record this amount in
  your* **profits table**.

Guess the weight

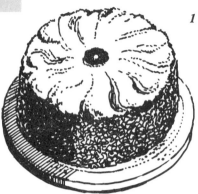

1 Carol's dad made a cake for a 'guess the weight' competition. It weighed 1220 g. Here are the guesses of 30 pupils.

500g 900g 1kg 450g 800g 2kg
920g 1200g 2kg 680g 1920g 1750g
1250g 880g 2100g 900g 870g 1460g 1000g
900g 1500g 2100g 1660g 920g 1100g 1300g
990g 1520g 920g 1000g

(a) Tom gave the best guess and won the cake. What was his guess?

(b) Each guess cost 10p. How much did the 30 pupils contribute altogether?

(c) Pupils who guessed within 100 g of the true weight had their 10p's returned. How much **profit** was made from the 30 pupils?

(d) The profit from **other** pupils in Gladeside School was £23·40. Record the **total** profit from the competition in your **profits table**.

2 Find how good your class is at estimating weight. Ask your teacher for the parcel. Write down your own estimate of its weight. Compare your class's estimates.
Who had the best estimate?

Lucy and Paul decided to make and sell
Chocolate Raisin Slices for three weeks
before the Gladeside Concert.

CHOCOLATE RAISIN SLICES

60 g butter	Melt butter and chocolate in a pan over a
250 g crushed digestive biscuits	low heat. Remove from heat and stir in raisins and condensed milk. Add crushed
120 g chocolate	biscuits and stir well. Press into
125 g raisins	medium sized baking tray. Cut into
small tin condensed milk	fingers when cold.

Ask your teacher if you may make this.

3 Use a calculator if you need to.
Their parents donated
nine 125 g packets of butter
sixteen 250 g packets of digestive biscuits
twelve 150 g bars of chocolate
eight 250 g packets of raisins
seventeen small tins of condensed milk.

(a) How many batches of the recipe can they make?

(b) One batch gives 16 slices. They sell each slice for 25p. What is the profit from one batch?

(c) What is the **total** profit from the sale of the Chocolate Raisin Slices? Record this amount in your **profits table.**

4 (a) Complete your **profits table** to find the grand total.

(b) Look at the four items on page 17. Decide which items Gladeside School should buy so that they have at least £150 left in the school fund.

(c) Find the total cost of these items and the amount left in the school fund.

Ask your teacher what to do next.

1 **You need a jar, two stones of different sizes and an elastic band.**
  (a) Put some water in the jar and mark the water level with the elastic band.
  (b) Put the smaller stone in the jar. What happens to the water level?
  (c) Take the stone out. What happens to the water level?
  (d) Put the larger stone in the jar. What do you notice?

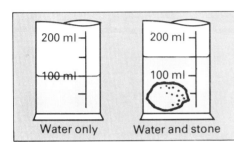

The difference between the two readings gives the volume of the stone in millilitres.
The volume of the stone is 150 − 100 = 50 ml

$$1 \text{ ml} = 1 \text{ cm}^3$$

The volume of the stone is 50 cm³

Water only   Water and stone

2 **You need a litre measuring jar, the two stones and other objects which sink.**

Copy and complete the table.

Object	Water only – level in ml	Water and object – level in ml	Volume of object in ml or cm³
Small stone			

3 Find the volume, **in cm³**, of the tomato, the egg and the carrot.

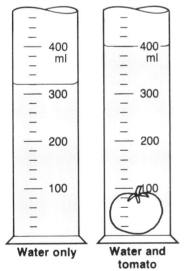

Water only   Water and tomato

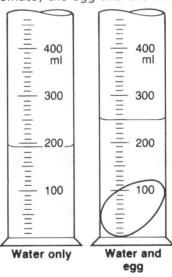

Water only   Water and egg

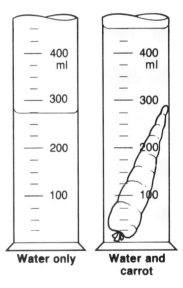

Water only   Water and carrot

4 A 1-litre measuring jar is filled to the 500 ml mark with water. To what mark on the jar would you expect the water to rise when each of these objects is submerged in the water?

(a)

Wash'n'Shine 75ml

(b)

Chocobloc
2 cm 6 cm 8 cm

(c)

Magi-Cube
5 cm

Ask your teacher what to do next.

Taking bearings at sea

1 Use the protractor you cut out from **Workbook page 22** or a circular protractor.
Place it in the circle on the map so that 000° lines up with the North direction.
Find the bearing of each place on the map from the *Lorne Queen*.
Record like this:

Place	Bearing
Millport	000°

2 On what bearing should the *Lorne Queen* sail to pick up survivors from
(a) a sailing dinghy at point **D**
(b) a fishing boat at point **F**?

3 On what bearing is the *Lorne Queen* sailing on the map?

4 Write down suitable bearings for the *Lorne Queen* to pass
(a) between Pladda Island and Ailsa Craig
(b) between Arran and Bute.

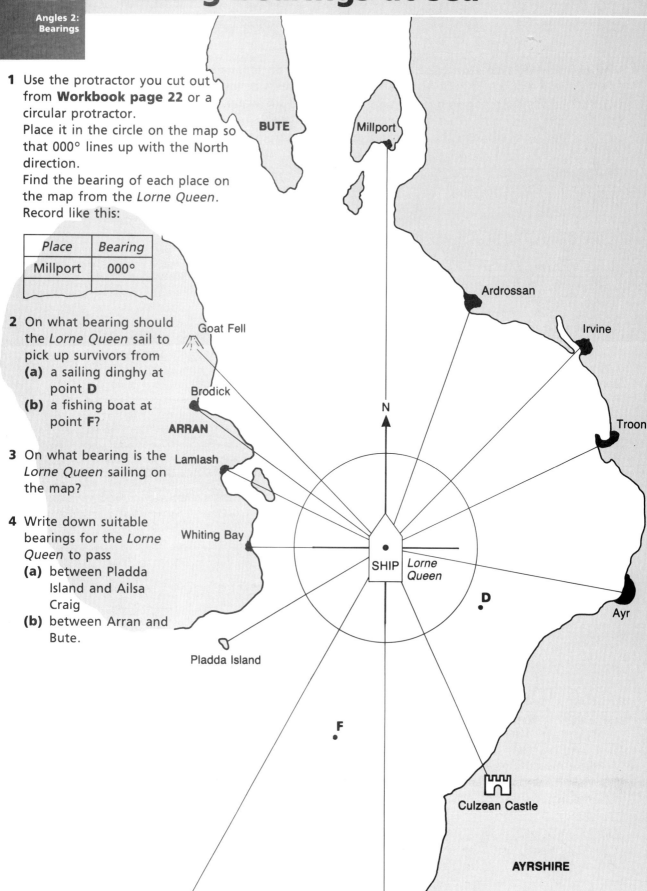

The thick line shows the *Vulture*'s course round Wreck Island. The scale is **1 cm to 1 km**.

	Distance	Bearing
A to B	7·5 km	300°
B to C		
C to D		
D to E		

1 Describe the journey from **A** to **E** using **distances** and **bearings**. Start by making a table like the one shown.

2 Make another table to describe the journey in reverse – from **E** back to **A**.

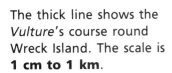

Wreck Island

Dark Island

Dead Man's Point

Scale: 1 cm to 1 km

3 The dotted lines show the flight paths of a helicopter.
Find the distance and bearing when it flies **(a)** from **A** to **C**
(b) from **E** to **B**
(c) from **D** to **A**.

Ask your teacher what to do next.

Friday 20th March

When Alan got home on Friday, he looked at the notice board in his bedroom.

He also read his diary for Friday and Saturday.

Ticket to admit **ONE** only
The SATURDAY YOUTH CLUB
Video Night
7.15 pm
21st March

ALAN
COLIN PHONED TO SAY HE NOW HAS A TICKET FOR THE Y.C. VIDEO NIGHT. HE AND JAMIE WILL MEET YOU OUTSIDE SANDRA LOW'S HOUSE AT QUARTER TO 7 ON SATURDAY
Mum
P.S. WHO IS SANDRA LOW ANYWAY?

DIARY

**20 MARCH
FRIDAY** Karate club 7.30
Snooker on T.V. at 10 to 9

**21 MARCH
SATURDAY** Gran's for lunch
Be there ¼ to 1.

Meet you Saturday 20 to 3 outside the Langton Street turnstiles. Colin can't make it. Jamie

JOHN ADAMS · Dental Surgeon
Dear Alan
Your next appointment is at 9.15am on 21st March

1 Describe the things Alan is likely to be doing on Friday night and Saturday, giving the times **in order**.

You could start like this:
**Friday 20th March   5.20 pm
Take pie out of oven.**

Friday 4 o'clock
Dear Birdbrain,
Don't forget to take the pie out of the oven at 5.20 or I'll exterminate you.
Your beautiful kind sister Nicola

FOOTBALL CHALLENGE
Ground **G4**
**ROVERS
V.
UNITED**
Saturday 21st March 3 pm

2 Alan's watch shows **24-hour time**. It also shows the day and date.

What do you think Alan would be doing at each of these times?

Date
Friday
20th March

Time
21.05
9.05 pm
five past nine at night

(a)

(b)

(c)

(d)

(e)

3 Write each of the times in question **2(b)** to **(e)** in two other ways.

4 Alan's favourite Saturday TV programmes are:

Saturday Club	10.00 to 13.00
Sports Report	16.25 to 18.00

Explain why he may not be able to see the whole of each programme.

Dierdre lives in Belfast. She asked her relations in Glasgow, Newcastle and London to find out the following information for a project. She made this table.

Sun
times of sunrise and sunset

Lights
times between which street lights and car lights must be on

Moon
times when the Moon rises and sets.

	Sun		Lights		Moon	
	rises	sets	on	off	rises	sets
Belfast	0759	1817	1847	0731	1833	1003
Glasgow	0756	1808	1838	0728	1819	1002
Newcastle	0743	1759	1829	0715	1813	0946
London	0731	1800	1830	0703	1823	0926

1 Name the city where
  (a) the Sun sets at six o'clock   **(b)** the Sun rises at four minutes to eight.
  (c) the Moon sets at three minues past ten.
  (d) the lights are switched on at twenty-two minutes to seven.

2 In which city does the Sun rise **(a)** earliest **(b)** latest?

3 In which city does the Sun set **(a)** earliest **(b)** latest?

4 In which month do you think Dierdre made this table – July, October or December?

5 (a) In Newcastle, how long is it after sunset when the lights are switched on?
  (b) Is this the same for the other cities?

6 (a) In Glasgow, how long is it after sunset when the Moon rises?
  (b) Is this the same for the other cities?

1759 and 1 minute is 1800. 1800 and 29 minutes is 1829 Altogether.....

7 How many minutes later does the Sun rise in Belfast than in London?

In Newcastle the Sun rises at 0743 which is about quarter to 8.

8 Give approximate times for

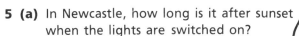

LONDON	
0731 sunrise	1800 sunset

  (a) sunset in Belfast
  (b) sunrise in London
  (c) the Moon setting in Glasgow
  (d) lights off in London.

7.30 to noon is 4½ hours. Noon to six o'clock is 6 hours. Altogether that's...

9 For about how many hours is the Sun in the sky over London?

10 For about how many hours is the Moon in the sky over London?

11 Look at the table. Is it possible to see the Sun and Moon in the sky at the same time?

Ask your teacher what to do next.

As time goes by

You need a diary or a calendar.

1 Mr and Mrs Brown celebrate their golden wedding this year.
 (a) In which year were they married?
 (b) On what day of the week will they celebrate their anniversary this year?

2 Find out what is meant by **(a)** a diamond wedding **(b)** a ruby wedding **(c)** a silver wedding.

3 In which year did Mr and Mrs Brown celebrate **(a)** their silver wedding **(b)** their ruby wedding?

4 In which year will they celebrate their diamond wedding?

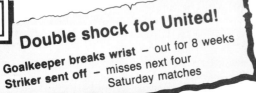

5 The game took place on the first Saturday of last September. Give the date of the Saturday for the return of **(a)** the goalkeeper **(b)** the striker.

Timeshare

ONE WEEK IS YOURS FOREVER!
Southern Spain, two room flat.
Week 32   Only £7400

6 What do you think this advertisement means?

7 In which month of the year do you think week 32 is?

8 For **Timeshare**, week 1 begins on the Saturday before (or on) 1st January.
 Use a calendar to find the date of the Saturday which begins week 32 this year.

9 Would the dates for week 32 be the same every year?

10 You want to be on holiday on your birthday this year.
 Which **Timeshare** week would you buy?

11 You buy week 32 at the price shown. You plan to use the flat for holidays until the year 2020.
 How much, to the nearest pound, will your holiday accommodation cost **per year**?

Ask your teacher what to do next.

Book Club Special

Each month the Book Club has a special offer.

1 (a) List all the possible choices from the **February** special.
Start like this:
   Birds and *The Reason*
(b) How many choices are there altogether?

JANUARY SPECIAL

THESE 2 BOOKS FOR £6.99

FEBRUARY SPECIAL

ANY 2 DIFFERENT BOOKS FOR £4.99

2 Sheona would like to buy two books from the **March** special.
(a) List her possible choices.
(b) How many choices does she have?
(c) She decides that *Dinosaurs* will be one of the books.
List her possible choices now.

MARCH SPECIAL

ANY 2 DIFFERENT BOOKS FOR £7.99

3 Check by listing that there are 10 possible ways of choosing 2 books from the **April** special.

APRIL SPECIAL

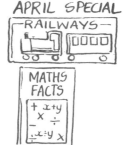

ANY 2 DIFFERENT BOOKS FOR £6.99

4 (a) Copy and complete the table.

	Jan	Feb	Mar	Apr
Number of choices	1			10

(b) Look at your table.
Describe the pattern.
(c) Use the pattern to predict the number of choices in the **May** special.
Check your answer by listing the possibilities.

MAY SPECIAL

ANY 2 DIFFERENT BOOKS FOR £5.99

5 The Book Club decides to let customers choose two copies of the same book as part of the special offer.
(a) Copy and complete this table to show how this decision would have affected the number of choices in the January to May specials.
(b) Describe the pattern in your table.
(c) How does this pattern compare with the one described in question **4(b)**?

	Jan	Feb	Mar	Apr	May
Number of choices	3				

Ask your teacher what to do next.

Sound Cellar

Marvin runs the Sound Cellar record shop. He drew this graph
to show
- the number of copies of different albums sold at the
  Sound Cellar **last** week
- the percentage change in the number of copies sold
  this week when compared to last week.

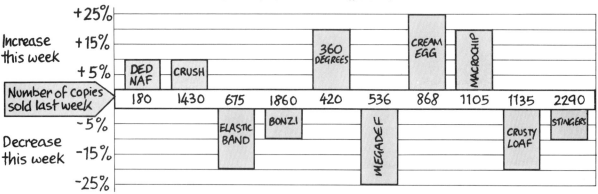

Sound Cellar - album sales

1 Last week Marvin sold 180 copies of Ded Naf's album. This
week he sold **10% more** copies. For each album give
(a) the number of copies sold last week.
(b) the percentage increase **or** decrease in copies sold this week.

> **This week**, how many
> copies of Ded Naf's
> album did Marvin sell?
>
> **Increase** in number sold = 10% of 180
> = $\frac{1}{10}$ of 180   (180 ÷ 10)
> = 18
> Number sold this week = 180 + 18 = **198**

2 For the albums by Crush, 360 Degrees, Cream Egg and
Macrochip, find for this week
(a) the increase in the number of copies sold
(b) the number of copies sold.

> **This week**, how many
> copies of Elastic Band's
> album did Marvin sell?
>
> **Decrease** in number sold = 20% of 675
> = $\frac{1}{5}$ of 675
> = 135
> Number sold this week = 675 − 135
> = **540**
>
> $5\overline{)675}$ = 135
>
> 675
> − 135
> **540**

3 For the albums by Bonzi, Megadef,
Crusty Loaf and Stingers, find, for this week
(a) the decrease in the number of
copies sold
(b) the number of copies sold.

Asif, Fiona and Tim collected some information from 200 people visiting the library.

1 Asif's tally sheet shows the replies to his question
'What type of book have you borrowed?'

18 out of the 200 he asked borrowed science fiction.

$$\frac{18}{200} = \frac{9}{100} = 9\%$$

9% borrowed science fiction.

What percentage of the people asked borrowed each of the other types of books?

Asif   20 March 1991

Books borrowed

Science fiction	⊣⊦⊦ ⊣⊦⊦ ⊣⊦⊦ |||
Crime	⊣⊦⊦ ⊣⊦⊦ ⊣⊦⊦ ⊣⊦⊦ ⊣⊦⊦ ⊣⊦⊦ ⊣⊦⊦	
Romance	⊣⊦⊦ ⊣⊦⊦ ⊣⊦⊦ ⊣⊦⊦ ⊣⊦⊦ ⊣⊦⊦ ⊣⊦⊦ ⊣⊦⊦ ||||
Horror	⊣⊦⊦ ⊣⊦⊦ ||
Adventure	⊣⊦⊦ ⊣⊦⊦ ⊣⊦⊦ ⊣⊦⊦ ⊣⊦⊦ |||
Others	⊣⊦⊦ ⊣⊦⊦ ⊣⊦⊦ ⊣⊦⊦ ||

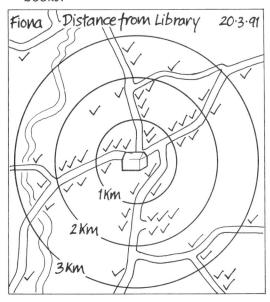

Fiona Distance from Library 20·3·91

1Km

2Km

3Km

2 Fiona asked 50 borrowers the question 'Where do you live?'
For each reply she placed a ✓ on the appropriate place on her map.

(a) For how many borrowers is the distance to the library
  ● less than 1 km
  ● between 1 km and 2 km
  ● between 2 km and 3 km
  ● more than 3 km?

(b) Express each answer in **(a)** as a percentage of the 50 borrowers questioned.

3 Tim estimated the age groups of 150 borrowers.
His grid shows this information.

48 out of the 150 are children.

$$\frac{48}{150} = \frac{96}{300} = \frac{32}{100}$$

32% are children.

(a) Find the total number in each of the other age groups.
(b) Express each number in **(a)** as a percentage of the 150 borrowers.

Ask your teacher what to do next.

Tim   Age Groups   20 March 1991
c-children T-Teenagers Y-Younger adults
      O-Older adults   P-Pensioners

C	C	Y	P	C	C	C	T	T	C	Y	T	C	Y	O
Y	Y	C	T	C	C	Y	T	C	C	Y	P	O	C	Y
Y	C	C	Y	C	Y	O	Y	T	T	T	Y	Y	T	T
T	Y	P	O	T	T	C	C	Y	C	Y	C	Y	Y	C
Y	C	Y	C	Y	Y	Y	T	T	C	C	Y	O	O	Y
Y	O	Y	P	C	Y	T	T	T	C	Y	Y	C	C	O
C	Y	Y	C	Y	O	C	C	Y	C	Y	C	Y	O	Y
Y	T	T	T	T	C	C	Y	Y	T	T	Y	P	C	Y
O	Y	C	C	Y	Y	C	O	T	Y	C	Y	T	T	Y
C	C	Y	Y	T	T	C	Y	C	Y	C	P	C	Y	T

Turning left and right

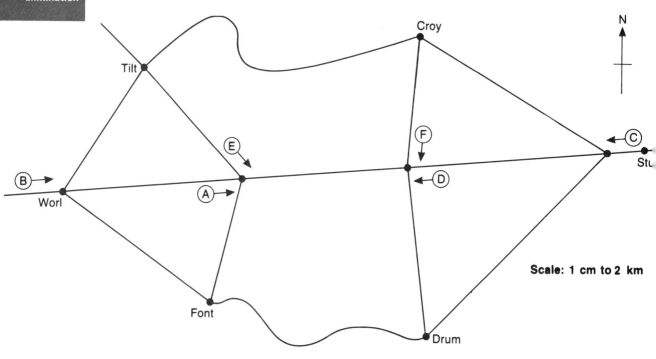

Cars (A), (B), (C), (D), (E) and (F) are approaching road junctions.
Each junction has a road sign. Some signs are broken.

1 Match each car to one of these road signs.
Record like this:

Car (A) ➝ Sign ☐

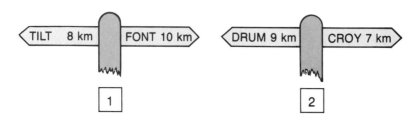

〈 TILT 8 km | FONT 10 km 〉	〈 DRUM 9 km | CROY 7 km 〉	〈 4 km | CROY 12 km 〉
1	**2**	**3**

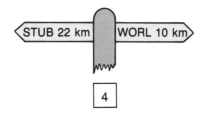
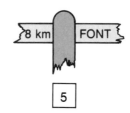

〈 STUB 22 km | WORL 10 km 〉	〈 8 km | FONT 〉	
4	**5**	**6**

2 Draw a complete road sign for

(a) the broken sign ☐ 6

(b) a car approaching the Worl–Stub road from the Southwest

(c) a car approaching Tilt from the Northwest.

Ask your teacher what to do next.

1 Route maps often show distances between towns.
The distance from Douglas to Ramsay is 15 miles

on this map and **in this distance table**.

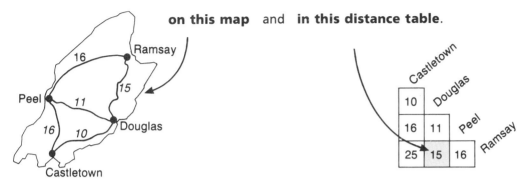

Use the distance table. What is the distance between
(a) Douglas and Peel   **(b)** Castletown and Ramsay
(c) Peel and Ramsay   **(d)** Peel and Castletown?

2 Find the shortest distances in miles between towns on each map.
Copy and complete each distance table.

(a)

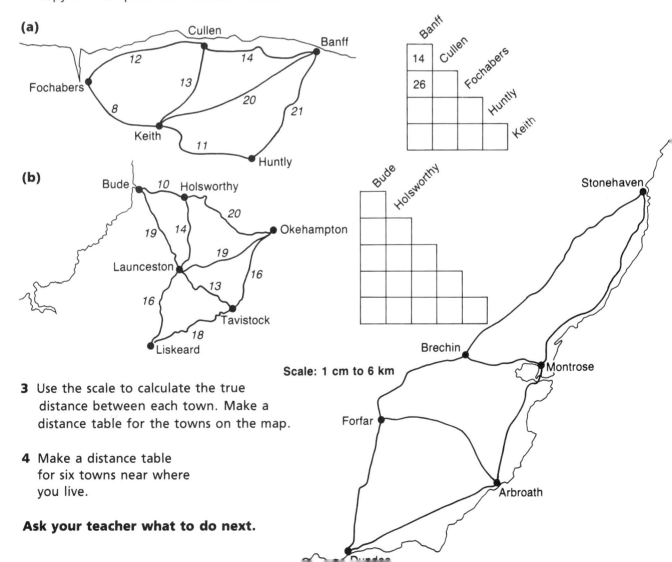

3 Use the scale to calculate the true
distance between each town. Make a
distance table for the towns on the map.

4 Make a distance table
for six towns near where
you live.

Ask your teacher what to do next.

Glenafton weather station

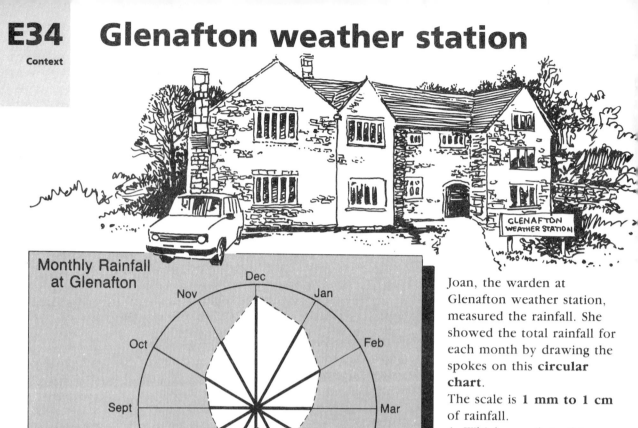

Monthly Rainfall at Glenafton

Joan, the warden at Glenafton weather station, measured the rainfall. She showed the total rainfall for each month by drawing the spokes on this **circular chart**.

The scale is **1 mm to 1 cm** of rainfall.

1 Which month in this chart had
   (a) most rain
   (b) least rain
   (c) about the same amount of rain as February
   (d) a total rainfall of 25 cm?

Joan showed some visiting pupils how to make a circular chart using a large paper circle.

Fold to quarter. Mark the points.

Fold flap to centre.

Mark the new points.

Fold flap to centre.

Mark the new points.

Lightly draw the six diameters.

---

2 Use the information in Joan's record table below.
   Make circular charts showing, for each month
   (a) the average maximum daily temperature
   (b) the average daily hours of sunshine.
   Choose a scale for the lengths of the spokes to suit the **greatest** monthly value.

	Jan	Feb	Mar	Apr	May	June	July	Aug	Sept	Oct	Nov	Dec
Average maximum daily temperature in °C	6·6	4·5	7·2	8·4	10·9	14·1	17·3	16·8	14·3	11·4	8·6	7·1
Average daily hours of sunshine	1·8	2·7	3·5	5·1	5·8	6·2	5·9	5·1	4·4	3·2	2·4	1·2

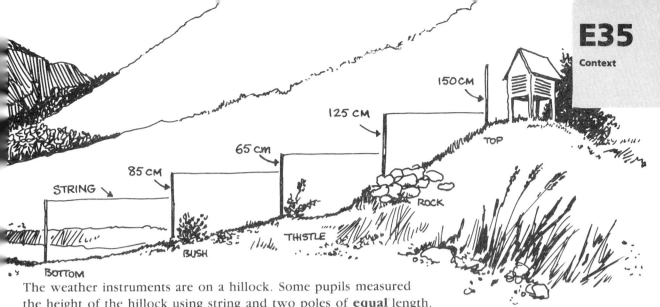

STRING
85 CM
65 cm
125 CM
150 CM
TOP
ROCK
THISTLE
BUSH
BOTTOM

The weather instruments are on a hillock. Some pupils measured
the height of the hillock using string and two poles of **equal** length.
The ground at the bush was 85 cm higher than the ground at the
bottom.

3 How much higher was
  (a) the ground at the thistle than the
    ground at the bush
  (b) the ground at the rock than the
    ground at the thistle
  (c) the ground at the thistle than the
    ground at the bottom?

4 What was the height of the hillock?

5 Use this method to find the height of a
    hillock near your school.

The pupils wondered how the wind vane had been positioned.
Joan explained one way of finding the direction of North.
  ● Shadows point North when the Sun is due South.
  ● The Sun is due South when it is at its highest in the sky.
  ● The Sun is highest mid-way between sunrise and sunset.
  ● You can find the time mid-way between sunrise
    and sunset like this:

Sunrise 7.30 am
Sunset 4.50 pm

> 7.30 to 12 is 4 hours 30 minutes
> 12 to 4.50 pm is 4 hours 50 minutes
> So 7.30 to 4.50 is 8 hours 80 minutes
> half this time is 4 hours 40 minutes

Shadows point
North at 12.10 which is 4 hours 40 minutes after 7.30 am.

6 For these days at what time do shadows
    point North?

	(a)	**(b)**
Sunrise	4.40 am	7.20 am
Sunset	9.50 pm	4.44 pm

7 Use this method to find the direction of
    North at your school.

Ask your teacher what to do next.

Abermore trout farm

1 A school party visited Abermore trout farm.
Morris the guide gave them lots of information.
They saw this graph about the average weight of trout at different ages.

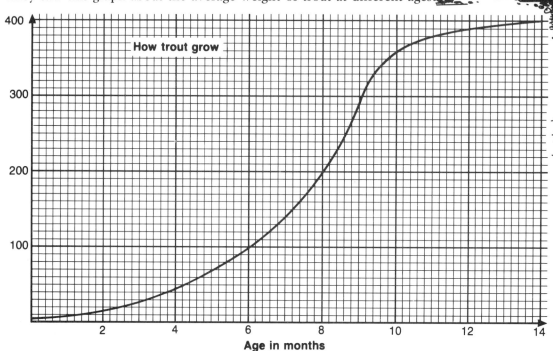

How trout grow

Weight in g

Age in months

(a) How old are trout weighing about 300 g?

(b) Trout weighing about 125 g are used to restock rivers and lakes for fishing.
About what age are these trout?

(c) During which of these months does a trout's weight increase the most?

2 Morris explained that, as a trout grows, you can eat a greater percentage of its weight.

20% of a 200g trout can be eaten   25% of a 400g trout can be eaten

For 200 g trout find   (a) the approximate age
(b) how many altogether weigh 2 kg
(c) what weight out of 2 kg can be eaten.

3 Repeat question **2** for 400 g trout.

4 Ten of the pupils decided to have trout for tea.
Give a reason for buying   (a) ten 200 g trout   (b) five 400 g trout.

5 To produce healthy trout the farm uses 8640 thousand litres
per day of clean running water. How many litres is this
(a) per hour (b) per minute (c) per second?

6 Morris told the pupils about one fish tank.
- It contained 8-month-old trout.
- It held 440 cubic metres of water.
- It contained 35 kg of trout **per cubic metre**.
- **(a)** What was the total weight of trout in the tank?
- **(b)** Use the graph to find the average weight of these trout.
- **(c)** About how many trout were in the tank?

The pupils asked if there was a way of finding the approximate
number of fish in Loch Abermore.
Morris explained one way to do this:
- Catch 100 fish, mark them and put them back.
- Allow time for the marked fish to mix thoroughly with the others.
- Catch 50 fish and count how many are marked.
- Suppose 3 are marked, calculate like this:

Marked fish	All fish
3	50
1	$50 \div 3 = 17$ to nearest whole fish
100	$17 \times 100 = 1700$

There are about 1700 fish altogether.

7 Your group could use this method to find approximately how
many beans there are in one kilogram:
- Mark 100 beans, put them back and mix **thoroughly**.
- Without looking, take out 50 beans.
- Count the numbers of beans which are marked ■
- Calculate like this:

Marked beans	All beans
■	50
1	$50 \div ■ = ●$ to the nearest whole number
Number marked at the start → 100	$● \times 100 = ?$

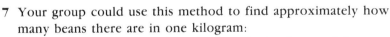

This last number is about the number
of beans in one kilogram.

Ask your teacher what to do next.

Some digit sums

1 (a) The sum of the two digits in
Sheena's age is 1+2 = **3**.
The **digit sum** is **3**.

Find two other ages for which
the sum of the two digits is 3.

(b) How old is Sheena's dad?

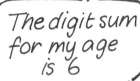

My age is an
even number
between 35 and 55

The digit sum
for my age
is 6

2 (a) List the multiples of 9 from 18 to 90.
(b) Find the digit sum for each multiple. What do you
notice?

3 Which two-digit number has
(a) the greatest digit sum? What is this sum?
(b) the smallest digit sum? What is this sum?

4 Find all the different two-digit numbers whose digit sum is **4**.

5 List all the different two-digit numbers whose digit sum is
(a) 5 **(b)** 2 **(c)** 1 **(d)** 6

6 Use your results from questions **1**, **4** and **5**.
Copy and complete this table.

Digit sum	1	2	3	4	5	6
Number of different two-digit numbers						

7 Find 6 different **three-digit** numbers whose digit sum is 3.

8 Investigate three-digit numbers whose digit sum is
(a) 1 **(b)** 2 **(c)** 4 **(d)** 5

Ask your teacher what to do next.

Page 1 Seeing stars
1 (d) The shape obtained is a regular octagon.
2 A star like the one shown on the textbook page.
3 (d) The shape obtained is a regular hexagon.
4 (a) (b) Designs and activity depend on the pupil's choice.

Page 2 Tile patterns
2 Many patterns are possible.
3 **(a)** AB, CD **(b)** AB, CD, EF, GH **(c)** GH
4 The patterns are symmetrical in **(a)** and **(b)**.
  (a) CF **(b)** PS, TQ, RU **(c)** not symmetrical

Page 3 Large wall patterns
1, 2, 3, 4 Practical work
5 **(a)** 6 lines of symmetry
  (b) Practical work

Page 4 Cars and racetracks
1 **(a)** 126 cm **(b)** 302·4 cm
2 **(a)** 64 cm **(b)** 70·4 cm
3 Answers depend on the models and scales used.
4 **(a)** 265 m **(b)** 625 m **(c)** 180 m
5 **(a)** about 320 m **(b)** about 200 m
  (c) about 540 m
6 **(a)** about 2·13 km **(b)** about 162 km

Page 5 Model houses
1 B 10 cm C 18 cm D 6 cm
  E 19 cm F 20 cm G 28 cm
  H 26 cm I 15 cm J 16 cm K 12 cm
2 Practical work

Page 6 Keeping warm
1 **(a)** 14 **(b)** 33 **(c)** 41 **(d)** 12
2 **(a)** walls **(b)** draughts
3 **(a)** 20% **(b)** 50% **(c)** 30%
4 **(a)** $\frac{1}{4}$ **(b)** $\frac{1}{10}$ **(c)** $\frac{1}{5}$ **(d)** $\frac{1}{2}$
5

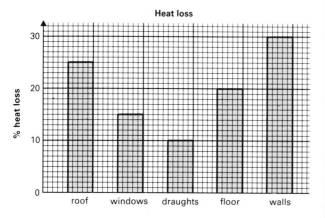

Heat loss

6 The pie chart (the quarter circle is obvious).

7

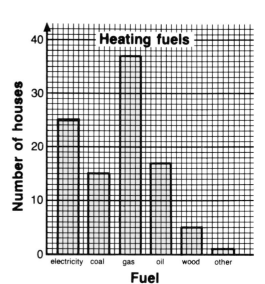

8 **(a)** bar graph **(b)** pie chart **(c)** bar graph
  (d) pie chart

Page 7 Putting 18 holes
1 **(b)** First nine holes

Score	Tally marks	Number of times
1	II	2
2	THL IIII	9
3	THL THL THL THL II	22
4	THL THL THL I	16
5	THL	5

2

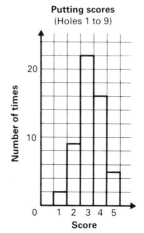

Putting scores
(Holes 1 to 9)

3 3
4 **(a)** 21 times **(b)** 10 times

5 (1)

Last nine holes

Score	Tally marks	Number of times
1	III	3
2	TH TH TH TH	20
3	TH TH TH TH I	21
4	TH III	8
5	II	2

Page 7   Putting 18 holes

5 (2)

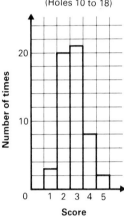

Putting scores
(Holes 10 to 18)

Number of times vs Score

(3)   3
(4)   **(a)** 10 times   **(b)** 23 times

6   Both graphs show that the most common score is 3. Their shapes are similar but the graph for holes 10 to 18 shows fewer higher scores (4s and 5s) and more lower scores (2s). Reasons for this could be discussed.

Page 8   Domino Squares

1   There is only one other arrangement.

6	6	3	6
6	6	4	4
5	5	3	5
5	5	3	4

2   Possible arrangements:

(a)

6	4	5	5
4	5	6	5
6	6	3	3
4	3	5	6

(b)

5	6	4	6
5	6	6	5
5	3	6	4
3	5	4	3

(c)

3	5	4	5
6	5	3	5
6	6	4	5
4	3	6	6

(d)

6	6	5	4
3	5	4	5
6	6	3	5
4	3	6	5

(e)

4	3	4	5
6	5	6	4
6	5	5	6
5	3	6	3

(f)

3	5	6	6
6	4	4	6
5	5	3	3
4	6	5	5

There are several possible answers for **(a)**, **(b)**, **(c)**, and **(e)**, two possible answers for **(f)**, and only one for **(d)**.

Page 9   Check it out

1   What Steve says is true.
2   What Lisa says is true.
3   **(a)** $7 \times 8 = 56$ $8 \times 7 = 56$
            $9 \times 13 = 117$ $13 \times 9 = 117$
            $14 \times 16 = 224$ $16 \times 14 = 224$
     (b) The answers to the multiplications for each pair are the same.
     (c) You can multiply two numbers in any order.
4   **(a)** $3 \times 4 \times 5 = 60$ $4 \times 5 \times 3 = 60$ $5 \times 3 \times 4 = 60$
            $8 \times 7 \times 9 = 504$ $7 \times 9 \times 8 = 504$ $9 \times 8 \times 7 = 504$
     (b) The answers to the multiplications in each set are the same.
     (c) You can multiply three numbers together in any order.
     (d) You can multiply four numbers together in any order.
5   What Aziz says is true.
6 $67 \div 5 = 13 \text{ r } 2$
     You can check a division with a remainder by multiplying your answer, 13, and the number you divided by, 5 (giving 65), then adding your remainder, 2 (giving 67 which is the number you divided).

Page 10   Split it!

1   Area of rectangle **P** $= 32 \text{ cm}^2$
     Area of rectangle **Q** $= \underline{10 \text{ cm}^2}$
     Area of **whole** shape $= \underline{42 \text{ cm}^2}$
2   **(a)** 22 cm^2 **(b)** 24 cm^2 **(c)** 22 cm^2 **(d)** 24 cm^2
3   **(a)** 14 cm^2 **(b)** 18 cm^2 **(c)** 21 cm^2
     (d) 25 cm^2 **(e)** 20 cm^2
4   Various answers are possible.

Page 11   Split it!

1   Area of rectangle $= 12 \text{ cm}^2$
     Area of triangle **X** $= 3 \text{ cm}^2$
     Area of triangle **Y** $= 1\frac{1}{2} \text{ cm}^2$
     Area of trapezium $= 16\frac{1}{2} \text{ cm}^2$
2   **(a)** 21 cm^2 **(b)** 21 cm^2 **(c)** 22 cm^2
3   **(a)** 18 cm^2 **(b)** 14 cm^2 **(c)** 14 cm^2 **(d)** 16 cm^2
     (e) 14 cm^2

Page 12   Costs and wages

1   Strawberry: 65p   Raspberry: 99p
     Blackcurrant: £1·10
2   Gooseberry: 5p cheaper   Blackberry: 15p cheaper
     Redcurrant: 15p cheaper
3   **(a)** 6·76   **(b)** 6·89   **(c)** 12·6   **(d)** 20·5
4   **(a)** £2·72   **(b)** £3·06   **(c)** £1·65   **(d)** £3·38
     (e) £3·91   **(f)** £3·20

Page 13 *Kitty* and *Hawk*
1 (a) 2 seconds   (b) $\frac{1}{2}$ metre
2 (a) 60 seconds   (b) 24 seconds   (c) 34 seconds
3 (a) 9 metres   (b) 7 metres   (c) $13\frac{1}{2}$ metres
4 (a) 16 metres   (b) 16 metres   (c) 16 metres
5 (a) The answers are the same.
   (b) The boat had stopped travelling.
6 (a) $\frac{1}{2}$ metre   (b) 18 metres
7 (a) 2 metres   (b) $3\frac{1}{2}$ metres   (c) $3\frac{1}{2}$ metres

8
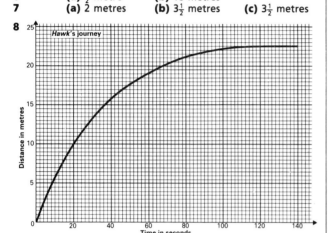

Page 14 Afternoon cruises
1 (a) 10 minutes   (b) 4 kilometres
2 (a) 1.30 pm   (b) 2.30 pm   (c) 3 pm
   (d) 3.30 pm   (e) 4.15 pm   (f) 5.45 pm
3 (a) 30 minutes   (b) 45 minutes
4 (a) 20 kilometres   (b) 20 kilometres
   (c) 32 kilometres   (d) 32 kilometres
5 (a) 12 kilometres   (b) 56 kilometres
6

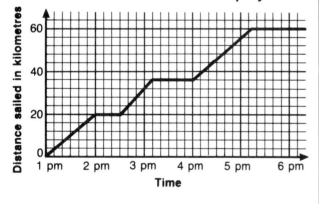

Page 15 Boats for hire
1 (a) Suresail: £12   Marina Craft: £15
   (b) Suresail: £32   Marina Craft: £30
2 If you wish to hire for less than 6 hours, it is
   cheaper to use Suresail.
   If you wish to hire for more than 6 hours, it is
   cheaper to use Marina Craft.
   For a time of 6 hours, the hire charge is the
   same.

3 (a)   **Suresail**

Time in hours	2	5	10
Cost in £	16	40	80

Marina Craft

Time in hours	2	5	10
Cost in £	22	37	62

(b)
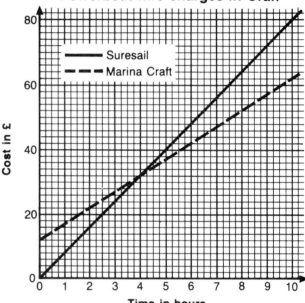

4 (a) Suresail charges less for 3 hours.
       Marina Craft charges less for 8 hours.
   (b) If you wish to hire for less than 4 hours, it is
       cheaper to use Suresail.
       If you wish to hire for more than 4 hours, it is
       cheaper to use Marina Craft.
       For a time of 4 hours, the hire charge is the
       same.

Page 16 Marquees and tents
   Practical work

Page 17 The School Concert
1 Discussion
2 After completion of the work on pages 17 to 22
   the profit is as shown.

Profits Table	
School fund balance	£148·00
Ticket sales	£403·20
Programme sales	£56·40
Kiosk profits	x
Guess the weight of the cake	£26·10
Chocolate raisin slices	£60·00
Donations	£25·00
Grand total	y

x Answer will vary depending on size of cup used
y Answers will vary depending on kiosk profits.

Pages 18, 19   How many seats in the hall?

1   The dimensions **X** cm and **Y** cm will depend on the decisions made by the pupils.

2   It is expected that there will be differences between the actual measurements and those of Gladeside School.

3   **(a)** True length, 28 m   True breadth, 20 m
     (b) 2 m
     (c) The seating areas are 16 m long and 7 m broad.

4   **(a)** 14 chairs in a row
     (b) 16 rows of chairs (a 17th row would project into the passage area)

5   448 people

6   £403·20

7   The scale drawing will depend on the dimensions of the school hall.

8   The number of people will depend on the actual dimensions of the school hall.

Page 20   Programme planning

1

Class	Item	Duration
5	● Dance team	7.15–7.20
4	Sketch	7.21–7.25
3	● Choir	7.26–7.32
6	Gymnastic display	7.33–7.40

2 Many solutions are possible, for example:

Class	Item	Duration
1	● Singing Game – 'The Rainbow'	7.15–7.17
2	Mime – 'Robots'	7.18–7.21
1	● Ballet – 'Animal Magic'	7.22–7.25
2	● Dance – 'Maggie's Movers'	7.26–7.30
5	Play – 'Haunted House'	7.32–7.47
3	● Festival Choir	7.48–7.54
4	Sketch – 'Dad's Tea'	7.55–7.59
5	● 'Mexican Carnival'	8.00–8.06

3   **(a)** £56·40
     (b) Designs will vary depending on the pupil.

Page 21   The Concert Kiosk

1   Money collected: nuts   £6·40
                        apples   £9·18
                        Total   £15·58

2   **(a)** 12p   **(b)** 22p

3   **(a)** 3p   **(b)** 3p

4   Profit from crisps = £4·32
     Profit from coke   = £3·60
     Total profit   = £7·92

5   Answer depends on the size of the plastic cup used.

6   **(a), (b)** Answers depend on the answer to question **5**.

7   Answer depends on the answer to question **6 (a)**. Profit from orange = Profit on one bottle multiplied by 18.

8   Total profit = £15·58 + £7·92 + profit from orange in question **7**.

Page 22   Guess the weight

1   **(a)** 1200 g   **(b)** £3
     (c) 10p was returned to each of 3 pupils (guessing 1200 g, 1250 g and 1300 g). Profit from 30 pupils = £2·70
     (d) Total profit recorded in profits table = £23·40 + £2·70 = £26·10

2   Answer depends on the pupils and the weight of the parcel.

3   **(a)** 15 batches (twelve 150 g bars of chocolate give 1800 g of chocolate 1 batch uses 120 g. Number of batches = 1800 ÷ 120 = 15)
     (b) Profit from one batch = £4
     (c) Total profit recorded in profits table = £60

4   **(a), (b), (c)** Answers will vary depending on the grand total and the choice made.

Page 23   That sinking feeling

1   **(a)** Practical work   **(b)** The water level rises.
     (c) The water is at the level of the elastic band.
     (d) The water level rises to a higher level than when the smaller stone was put in the jar.

2   Answers depend on the objects chosen.

3   Tomato: 80 cm³   Egg: 60 cm³   Carrot: 175 cm³

4   **(a)** 575 ml mark   **(b)** 596 ml mark
     (c) 625 ml mark

Page 24   Taking bearings at sea

1

Place	Bearing
Millport	000°
Ardrossan	020°
Irvine	045°
Troon	065°

Place	Bearing
Ayr	100°
Culzean Castle	155°
Girvan	180°
Ailsa Craig	210°

Place	Bearing
Pladda Island	240°
Whiting Bay	270°
Lamlash	295°
Brodick	305°
Goatfell	315°

2   **(a)** 120°   **(b)** 195°

3   000°

4   **(a)** 215° or 220° or 225° or 230° or 235°
     (b) 325° or 330° or 335°
         or any bearing from 215° to 235°
         or any bearing from 325° to 335°

Page 25   Setting a course

1

	Distance	Bearing
A to B	7·5 km	300°
B to C	6·5 km	345°
C to D	9 km	030°
D to E	10·5 km	135°

2

	Distance	Bearing
E to D	10·5 km	315°
D to C	9 km	210°
C to B	6·5 km	165°
B to A	7·5 km	120°

3

	Distance	Bearing
A to C	about 13 km	320°
E to B	about 12 km	235°
D to A	about 18 km	170°

Page 26 Friday 20th March

1
    Friday 20th March
    5.20 pm   Take pie out of oven
    7.30 pm   Karate Club
    8.50 pm   Snooker on TV
    Saturday 21st March
    9.15 am   Dentist
    12.45 pm Lunch at Gran's
    2.40 pm   Meet Jamie at turnstiles
    3.00 pm   Football match
    6.45 pm   Meet Colin and Jamie at Sandra's house
    7.15 pm   Youth Club Video Night

2
(a) Watching snooker on TV
(b) Having lunch at Gran's
(c) Watching football match
(d) Sitting at the dentist's
(e) Going to the Karate Club

3
(a) 9.05 pm   five past nine at night
(b) 1.00 pm   one o'clock in the afternoon
(c) 3.35 pm   twenty-five to four in the afternoon
(d) 9.24 am   twenty-four minutes past nine in the morning
(e) 7.20 pm   twenty past seven in the evening

4
Alan might miss the first part of 'Saturday Club' because he is still at the dentist's. He will miss the last part of it because he is going to his Gran's for lunch. He is likely to miss the start of 'Sports Report' because the football match, Rovers v. United, will not finish until after 16.25.

Page 27 Sun and Moon

1 (a) London   (b) Glasgow   (c) Belfast
   (d) Glasgow
2 (a) London   (b) Belfast
3 (a) Newcastle   (b) Belfast
4 October
5 (a) 30 min   (b) Yes
6 (a) 11 min   (b) No
7 28 min
8 (a) About quarter past 6   (b) About half past 7
   (c) About 10 o'clock   (d) About 7 o'clock
9 About $10\frac{1}{2}$ hours
10 About 15 hours
11 Yes, in all four cities in the morning.

Page 28 As time goes by

1 (a), (b) Answers depend on the current year.
2 (a) Married for 60 years (b) Married for 40 years
   (c) Married for 25 years
3, 4 Answers depend on the current year.
5 (a), (b) Answers depend on the current year.
6 For a total cost of £7400 you can have a holiday in the flat in Spain for one week every year. The week available is the 32nd week in the year.
7 August (at least partly – see question **8**)
8 Answer depends on the current year.
9 No
10 Answer depends on the date of the pupil's birthday.
11 Answer depends on the current year.

Page 29 Book Club Special

1 (a) *Birds* and *The Reason*
   Birds and *Easy Sewing*
   The Reason and *Easy Sewing*
   (b) 3 choices
2 (a) *Just Joan* and *Easy Cooking*
   Easy Cooking and *Household Plants*
   Just Joan and *Household Plants*
   Easy Cooking and *Dinosaurs*
   Just Joan and *Dinosaurs*
   Household Plants and *Dinosaurs*
   (b) 6 choices
   (c) 3 choices: *Just Joan* and *Dinosaurs*
   Easy Cooking and *Dinosaurs*
   Household Plants and *Dinosaurs*
3 *Atlas* and *Railways*
   Atlas and *Maths Facts*
   Atlas and *101 Activities*
   Atlas and *Bertie's First Date*
   Railways and *Maths Facts*
   Railways and *101 Activities*
   Railways and *Bertie's First Date*
   Maths Facts and *101 Activities*
   Maths Facts and *Bertie's First Date*
   101 Activities and *Bertie's First Date*
4 (a)

	Jan	Feb	Mar	Apr
Number of choices	1	3	6	10

(b) The increase in the number of choices each month is one more than the increase in the number of choices in the previous month. Other descriptions are possible.
(c) 15 choices in the May special:
Cartoon Mixture and *Alien From Mars*
Origami and *Who?*
Cartoon Mixture and *Origami*
Origami and *High Fashion*
Cartoon Mixture and *Who?*
Origami and *Dictionary*
Cartoon Mixture and *High Fashion*
Who? and *High Fashion*
Cartoon Mixture and *Dictionary*
Who? and *Dictionary*
Alien From Mars and *Origami*
High Fashion and *Dictionary*
Alien From Mars and *Who?*
Alien From Mars and *High Fashion*
Alien From Mars and *Dictionary*

5 (a)

	Jan	Feb	Mar	Apr	May
Number of choices	3	6	10	15	21

(b) The increase in the number of choices each month is one more than the increase in the number of choices in the previous month. Other descriptions are possible.
(c) It is the same pattern except that it begins at 3 instead of 1.

Page 30 Sound Cellar

1

	Ded Naf	Crush	Elastic Band	Bonzi	360 Degrees
(a) Number of copies sold last week	180	1430	675	1860	420
(b) Percentage increase/ decrease this week	10% increase	10% increase	20% decrease	10% decrease	20% decrease

	Megadef	Cream Egg	Macrochip	Crusty Loaf	Stingers
(a) Number of copies sold last week	536	868	1105	1135	2290
(b) Percentage increase/ decrease this week	25% increase	25% decrease	20% increase	20% decrease	10% decrease

2

	Crush	360 Degrees	Cream Egg	Macrochip
(a) Increase in copies sold	143	84	217	221
(b) Number of copies sold	1573	504	1085	1326

3

	Bonzi	Megadef	Crusty Loaf	Stingers
(a) Decrease in copies sold	186	134	227	229
(b) Number of copies sold	1674	402	908	2061

Page 31 Library survey

1 Crime: 18%   Romance: 42%   Horror: 6%
Adventure: 14%   Others: 11%

2

	(a) Number of borrowers	**(b)** Percentage of borrowers
● less than 1 km	9	18%
● between 1 km and 2 km	23	46%
● between 2 km and 3 km	11	22%
● more than 3 km	7	14%
	50	100%

3

	(a) Number in age group	**(b)** Percentage of borrowers
C – Children	48	32%
T – Teenagers	30	20%
Y – Younger adults	54	36%
O – Older adults	12	8%
P – Pensioners	6	4%
	150	100%

Page 32 Turning left and right

1 Car (A) → Sign 5   Car (B) → Sign 1
Car (C) → Sign 3   Car (D) → Sign 2
Car (E) → Sign 4   Car (F) → Sign 6

2 **(a)**

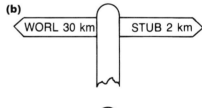
STUB 13 km   WORL 19 km

(b)

WORL 30 km   STUB 2 km

(c)

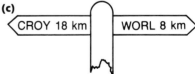
CROY 18 km   WORL 8 km

Page 33 Back to my routes

1   **(a)** 11 miles   **(b)** 25 miles   **(c)** 16 miles
    (d) 16 miles

2   **(a)**   **(b)**

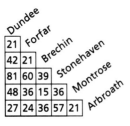

Other distance tables
are possible.

3

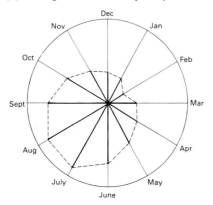

Other distance tables are possible.

4   Distance table depends on pupil's choice of towns.

Pages 34, 35 Glenafton weather station

1   **(a)** December   **(b)** June   **(c)** November
    (d) January

2   **(a)** Average maximum daily temperature

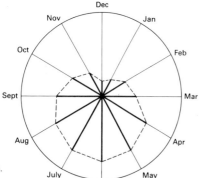

(b) Average daily hours of sunshine

Note:
The size of the
pupils' graphs
will depend on
the scales chosen.

---

3   **(a)** 65 cm   **(b)** 125 cm
    (c) 65 cm + 85 cm = 150 cm or 1 m 50 cm

4   150 cm + 125 cm + 85 cm = 425 cm or
    4 m 25 cm

5   Practical work

6   **(a)** 1.15 pm   **(b)** 12.02 pm

7   Practical work

Pages 36, 37 Abermore trout farm

1   **(a)** About 9 months old.
    (b) Between $6\frac{1}{2}$ and 7 months old.
    (c) From 8 to 9 months old (during the
    9th month).

2   **(a)** About 8 months old.
    (b) Ten 200 g trout weigh 2 kg.
    (c) 20% of 2 kg = 400 g

3   **(a)** About 14 months old.
    (b) Five 400 g trout weigh 2 kg.
    (c) 25% of 2 kg = 500 g

4   **(a)** Each pupil would get a whole trout.
    (b) Each pupil would get a greater weight
    (50 g rather than 40 g) to eat.

5   **(a)** 360 000 litres per hour
    (b) 6000 litres per minute
    (c) 100 litres per second

6   **(a)** 15 400 kg   **(b)** 200 g   **(c)** 77 000 trout

7   Practical work

Page 38 Some digit sums

1   **(a)** 21 years old and 30 years old
    (b) 42 years old

2   **(a)** 18, 27, 36, 45, 54, 63, 72, 81, 90
    (b) The digit sum for each multiple is 9.

3   **(a)** 99 has the greatest digit sum, 18
    (b) 10 has the smallest digit sum, 1

4   13, 22, 31, 40

5   **(a)** 14, 23, 32, 41, 50   **(b)** 11, 20   **(c)** 10
    (d) 15, 24, 33, 42, 51, 60

6

Digit sum	1	2	3	4	5	6
Number of different two-digit numbers	1	2	3	4	5	6

7   102, 111, 120, 201, 210, 300

8   **(a)** 100   **(b)** 101, 110, 200
    (c) 103, 112, 121, 130, 202, 211, 220, 301, 310,
    400
    (d) 104, 113, 122, 131, 140, 203, 212, 221, 230,
    302, 311, 320, 401, 410, 500